FROM HALDON
TO
MID-DARTMOOR
IN OLD PHOTOGRAPHS

BOWERMAN'S NOSE, NEAR MANATON, C. 1900. This great granite stack, 21 ft 6 in high, 'which Nature has rudely moulded into a semblance of the human form' (Crossing), is the eroded remnant of a tor, and one of the moor's most famous landmarks. Opinions vary as to the origins of the name!

FROM HALDON
TO
MID-DARTMOOR
IN OLD PHOTOGRAPHS

COLLECTED BY

TIM HALL

ALAN SUTTON
1990

Alan Sutton Publishing Limited
Phoenix Mill · Far Thrupp · Stroud · Gloucestershire

First Published 1990

British Library Cataloguing in Publication Data

From Haldon to Mid-Dartmoor in old photographs.
1. Devon. Dartmoor, history
I. Hall, Tim
942.3′53

ISBN 0-86299-609-0

For Sue, Nicholas and Jonathon – and in memory of Nigel Hollis

Typeset in 9/10 Korinna.
Typesetting and origination by
Alan Sutton Publishing Limited.
Printed in Great Britain by
Dotesios Printers Limited.

CONTENTS

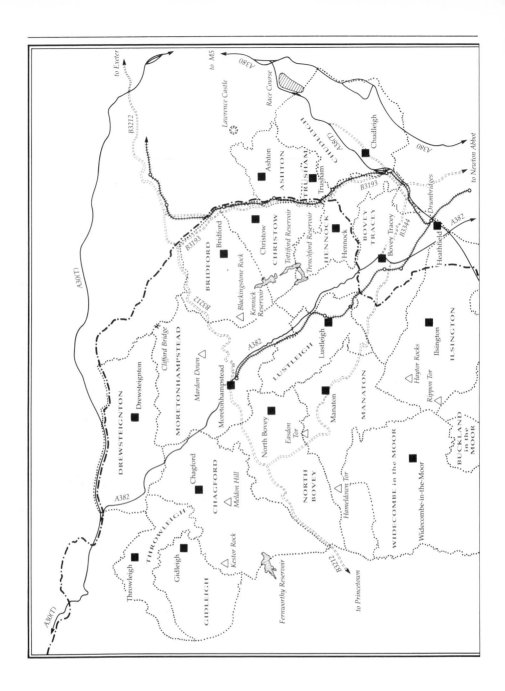

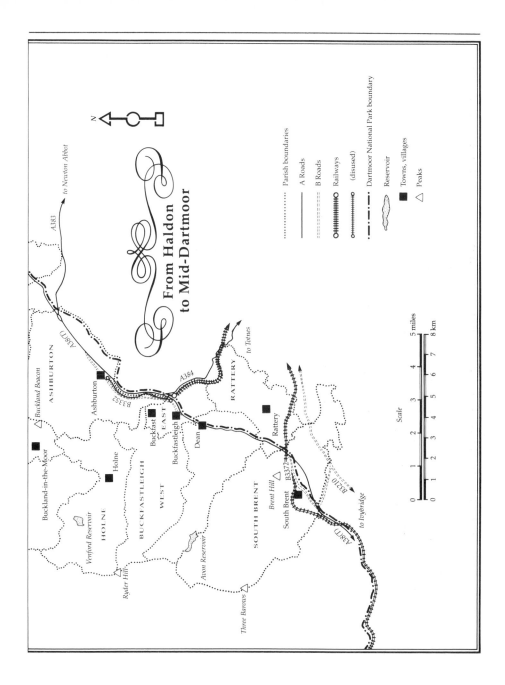

From Haldon to Mid-Dartmoor

N

to Newton Abbot

A383

Buckland Beacon △

ASHBURTON

A38(T)

Buckland-in-the-Moor ■

Holne ■

HOLNE

Venford Reservoir

Ryder Hill △

BUCKFASTLEIGH

WEST

Avon Reservoir

Three Barrows △

Ashburton ■

B3352

Buckfast ■

EAST

Buckfastleigh ■

Dean ■

A384

SOUTH BRENT

Brent Hill △

South Brent ■

B3372

RATTERY

Rattery ■

to Totnes

B3210

to Ivybridge

A38(T)

| Parish boundaries |
| A Roads |
| B Roads |
| Railways |
| (disused) |
| Dartmoor National Park boundary |
| Reservoir |
| ■ Towns, villages |
| △ Peaks |

Scale

0   1   2   3   4   5 miles
0   1   2   3   4   5   6   7   8 km

INTRODUCTION

The photographs in this book cover a roughly triangular area of beautiful Devonshire countryside lying between the Haldon Hills and the uplands of mid-Dartmoor. It is bounded on the north by the A30 and Teign Valley, and on the south by the A38. At the easternmost point is Chudleigh, whose parish rises up the slopes of Haldon. The western boundary is marked by a line from South Brent through the heart of the moor to the parishes of Throwleigh and Drewsteignton at the northern apex.

It has traditionally been a land of small farms, villages and market towns, of moorlands, wooded valleys and deep lanes, and of quarries, mines and small-scale industries. The photographs have been grouped to illustrate these characteristic features. Much of the region lies within the borders of the Dartmoor National Park – with the significant exception of the Bovey Tracey and Chudleigh districts – and is unsuited to large-scale, intensive farming methods. Indeed, the moor is often referred to as the last wilderness in southern England, and although it has been used for thousands of years – and continues to be so – large stretches remain uninhabited. Consequently, many of the pictures reveal landscapes and settlements that have changed less than most.

The earliest photograph included here dates from the 1870s (Chudleigh market place, page 111); the latest from 1976 (the demolition of the CWS woollen-mill chimney in Buckfastleigh, page 107). On the geological time-scale a century is nothing, a mere blip. Dartmoor itself, the 'Great Source' of Devon's rivers and building stone (as the historian W.G. Hoskins described it), assumed its present form over millions of years. People began to populate it a few thousand years ago, leaving behind a wealth of prehistoric remains.

Yet the subjects of many of the photographs – the farm workers pitching corn on to the horse-drawn wagons at harvest time; the steam train pulling out of a branch line station; the village children lined up in their best for the school photograph, boys in hob-nailed boots, girls in pinafores – sometimes seem as remote and as lost in time as those ancient moorland monuments. This impression is somehow reinforced by the photographs themselves. They reveal much about the past, but they can also mislead by freezing the moment, giving us the illusion that these people led lives of permanence and stability.

In fact, at the time the book's first picture was taken, the upheavals of the Industrial Revolution – one of the great shifts in world history – had already been felt in Devon. Although rural, Devon was not isolated from the wider economy. For example, from medieval times onwards, much of the county's prosperity had been founded on the sale of its woollen cloth in national and international markets. The trade was extensive and locally based, a true cottage industry. Throughout the region, a wide network of outworkers spun the wool from Dartmoor and Teign Valley sheep into yarn, and numerous small fulling (or tucking) mills, drawing on plentiful supplies of water from the upland streams to drive the machinery, wove the yarn into cloth. However, the introduction of steam-powered machinery into the woollen mills of Yorkshire in the eighteenth and early nineteenth centuries, using coal from large local reserves, meant that the northern companies could produce cloth far more cheaply than their rivals. The Devon mills were unable to compete, and by 1850 the vast majority were out of business.

The human cost was enormous: in homes, villages and towns throughout the area, from Chudleigh to Moretonhampstead, from Ashburton to Chagford, men and women had to make momentous decisions. Should they stay and try to find one of the scarce jobs, or ought they to risk moving to one of the growing towns like Exeter, Plymouth or Torquay, where opportunities were greater? Many decided to leave.

Thus, while many of our villages are probably just as attractive as they were in the mid-nineteenth century – and are certainly cleaner and healthier – their economic base has altered tremendously. This is in line with rural experience elsewhere, and may be summed up in one word: depopulation. In a host of parishes, Christow and Holne, Gidleigh and Manaton for example, there were fewer inhabitants in 1961 than there had been in 1851. Throughout that period many labourers and craftsmen, traders and shopkeepers – the living heart of the old communities – left the villages, and the carnage of two World Wars accelerated the process. It happened for a variety of reasons: farm mechanization, job obsolescence, the substitution of mass-produced goods for craftsmen's products, better communications, the desire for better-paid jobs in the towns, and so on.

Of course, many of the surnames listed in the old directories (for 1878, 1910, etc.) are still common in the district. Narracombe Farm near Ilsington has been in the hands of the Wills family for fourteen generations, and some of their farm workers notched up long periods of service (see page 23). Ilsington parish, like nearby Lustleigh, actually increased its population, acquiring a reputation as an attractive holiday and retirement area. More recently still, the widespread use of cars has led to the revival of many villages as desirable commuting bases.

Like everything else, farming has changed, shedding labour, increasing the use of machinery and amalgamating holdings. In 1801 the bulk of the county's population depended on agriculture for a living. A hundred years later, at a time when over three-quarters of a labourer's wage was spent on food, it still formed the largest single occupation. However, by the 1920s the holiday industry, with all its attendant shopkeepers, hoteliers and other trades, had become Devon's largest and most lucrative business. Nowadays, farming remains the dominant form of land use in the district, but it employs only thirteen per cent of the population.

The modern pressures on Dartmoor can be seen mounting from the mid-nineteenth century. Military training on the moor started in 1870, and the first of several reservoirs in what is now the national park was built at Tottiford in 1861 to supply an expanding Torquay. The large-scale planting of forests began after the First World War. Possible encroachments on common land, and the vulnerability of many of the prehistoric antiquities, also bothered many. Such threats increased people's awareness of the need to understand and conserve the moor, and the Dartmoor Preservation Association was founded in 1883. One of its first secretaries was Robert Burnard, an early advocate of national-park status for the moor. Many of his photographs appear in this book. The invaluable Dartmoor writings of William

Crossing (1847–1928) date from this time, and tourists began to visit the moor in growing numbers, enjoying more leisure time and better communications.

The industries illustrated here are all traditional in the sense that they drew on the region's natural resources: wool, clay, minerals and other rocks. We have already looked at the fate of the woollen industry; only in Buckfastleigh and Buckfast did it survive the harsh new economic climate. Tin mining, the other great historic industry of Dartmoor, continued at Birch Tor & Vitifer and Golden Dagger mines until the early twentieth century, but on nothing like the scale of former times. All the other mineral mines have closed, as have the quarries of the Teign Valley except at Trusham. The large ballclay deposits of the Bovey basin are still worked extensively, but only to the south of the area under discussion here.

The fortunes of the district's towns varied during this period, depending on location and local initiatives. Many continued to hold cattle markets, but the income from these diminished as facilities were centralized in Newton Abbot and Ashburton. Chagford, an old stannary and wool town, successfully promoted itself after the mid-nineteenth century as a moorland holiday resort. Chudleigh, also a former wool town, and an important staging post for coaches on the main road between Exeter and Plymouth, was badly hit by the opening of the South Devon railway in the 1840s. Overnight, the stage-coaches stopped running and the income dried up. Ashburton was affected in exactly the same way. Bovey Tracey, however, had over three hundred people employed in its pottery, which continued successfully until fairly recently. In Buckfastleigh, owing to the energies and foresight of the Hamlyns, the woollen mills adapted to the new challenges, and in 1890 there were still five mills at work. Railway traffic from the town was exceeded only by that at Plymouth, Exeter and Torre! The last mill closed in the 1970s.

Underlying many of these changes was a transport revolution. The coming of the branch railways after the 1860s effectively broke down much of the rural seclusion. Cecil Torr (author of *Small Talk at Wreyland*) noted how his grandfather stopped used a sundial and consulted the station clock instead. He had also complained about the 100 navvies who had terrorized Lustleigh in November 1864 with their drunken brawling. Torr himself died in 1928, having lived long enough to grumble about tourists in motor cars, to see the first aeroplane fly over Lustleigh (in 1918) and to view the first film made there – a Western, no less! It is a mark of how far we have come in such a short time that the 'revolutionary' steam locomotive should now be held in such nostalgic affection.

SECTION ONE

The Villages and Hamlets

THE GREEN, NORTH BOVEY, C. 1910. At that time the village supported a mixed elementary school (average attendance, fifty) and could call upon the services of a blacksmith, two millers, a carpenter, a postmaster-cum-bootmaker, a shopkeeper – and of course those of Miss Eliza Colridge, the publican of the Ring of Bells. Tin mining still continued in the west of the parish at Birch Tor & Vitifer (near the Warren House Inn).

ROWELL COTTAGES, CHUDLEIGH, C. 1925. The building dates back in part to the Middle Ages, and in the late seventeenth century a local highwayman, Jack Withrington, is said to have found refuge there. It is now a pub, appropriately named the Highwayman's Haunt.

THE COBLEY FAMILY AT ROWELL, CHUDLEIGH, C. 1890. The father, John Cobley, was a worker on Hamlyn's Farm, the home farm of the Whiteway estate, and in this group portrait he can be seen standing in the doorway in his working clothes. The rendering has come away around the barn door, revealing the wall's traditional cob construction.

THE COBLEY FAMILY AT ROWELL, C. 1895. Taken a few years after the previous picture, there are some obvious newcomers! Everyone is smartly dressed for the occasion, so perhaps John Cobley was progressing well at work.

CHRISTOW, C. 1910. It looks peaceful enough, but the hills and valleys around were busy with men working the farms, quarries and mines.

CHRISTOW, C. 1900. A cottage in the heart of this old village on the west side of the Teign. Apart from the horse and wagon the scene looks much the same today, although elsewhere in the village there has been a lot of new building.

HENNOCK, C. 1900. The village stands some 600 ft above sea level, the centre for a hilly parish between the Teign and Bovey valleys. At the time of the photograph there were two pubs in Hennock, the Union Inn and the Palk Arms. Men found work at Great Rock mine (see pages 97–99) or on one of the farms like Riley Farm, Crockham Farm, Lea Farm or Longlands. The nearby Trusham quarries (see page 100) opened in around 1906. Teign village, below Hennock, was built by the quarry company in 1910 to house extra workers.

LUSTLEIGH MAY DAY PROCESSION, c. 1910. The festival had died out in the village, but in the early twentieth century it was revived by Cecil Torr of Wreyland. In his classic *Small Talk at Wreyland* he wrote, 'the procession winds along through Lustleigh and through Wreyland, halting at certain places to sing the customary songs, and at last ascends the hill behind here [to Long Tor].'

THE LUSTLEIGH MAY QUEEN AT LONG TOR, 1932. Brenda Osborne was the queen that year; Joan Bourne (now Joan Ellis) is on the far left of the group. Today the enthronement and dancing take place in the Town Orchard.

MAY DAY DANCERS, LUSTLEIGH, 1912. After the procession, and the crowning and enthrone-ment of the May Queen at Long Tor, the twenty-four dancers performed their dance before her.

TUDOR MEMORIAL CROSS, LUSTLEIGH, c. 1910. It was erected in memory of Henry Tudor, rector from 1888 to 1904. The granite trough, still there today, is all that remains of the village's water pump. Note the condition of the rendering on the cottage wall, the long grass, and the elm tree (cut down c. 1950). Traditionally, the green was known as the town-place.

LUSTLEIGH SCHOOL, 1907. Mark Germon is at the top left, and Dorothy Hatherley is fourth from right in the second row. Mrs Menhenett was the teacher. A small charity school had opened in the village in 1825 (in what is now the Old Vestry), but it closed down after the introduction in 1870 of compulsory elementary education, and the construction of the new school. Declining numbers led to the closure of this school in the early 1960s. Cecil Torr lamented the arrival of universal education, saying that 'real country life is dying out – an unforeseen result of Education Acts.'

THE GREEN AT LUSTLEIGH, C. 1940. This is the oldest part of the village, although the steeply pitched tiled roof belongs to a Victorian house, one of the many that were built around the parish after the coming of the railway in 1866.

Lustleigh, Old Cottage.

WREYLAND MANOR, LUSTLEIGH, C. 1910. Formerly known as Hall House, this fine building dates back to the 1360s, although a date over the door records the alterations that were made to it in 1680. According to Cecil Torr, it was traditionally the home of the lords of Wreyland Manor. At the time the photograph was taken it was divided into three cottages.

LUSTLEIGH HOME GUARD, c. 1943. The picture was taken outside the village hall. Top row, from left: Peter Horrell, Percy Bunclark, Fred Baker, Jack Horrell, Bob Bourne, Ronnie Wills, Michael Morecombe, Fred Willcocks, Ronald Tremlett, Jim Knight, Jack Easton. Second row: George Reed, Harold Wills, Fred Aggett, Mr Phelps, Mr Humphreys, Godfrey Lockyear, Richard Walford, Tom Lockyear, Mr Jones, Mr Mocock. Front row: Harold Olding, Capt Stock, Mr Farrell, Jack Gould, Bill Laxton, Ernest Olding (with Sten gun), Ernest Squires, Richard Bourne. On the ground at left is a Vickers machine-gun, and at right a Lewis gun.

LUSTLEIGH, c. 1950. Riders leaving the village in the Rudge direction. At front left is Miss Mavis Covernton, now Mrs Cripps of Easton Cross, Chagford; she ran a riding stables at Caseley. The clock on the church tower was given by her mother in memory of her late husband.

LUSTLEIGH BELL-RINGERS, c. 1930. From left to right are: George Morecombe, Tom Payne (the 'captain of the tower' and the village blacksmith), Tom Coles, Sylvester Morecombe, Lewin Hill, Mark Germon, Jacob Wright, Richard Bourne. Cecil Torr wrote of the Lustleigh bells, 'when I was young, the church bells said Crock, Kettle and Pan . . . there are more bells now, and they say something else – all swear words, I believe.'

ILSINGTON VILLAGE, c. 1900. The photograph shows the only shop and post office, kept by Susan Cumming. To the left of the picture can be seen the shute for collecting the only available water, which ran down from Haytor in an open gutter. Further up the village can be seen the old linhay with mounting steps outside, and by the church entrance the oil lamp lit by hand every evening, erected by parishioners to commemorate the Golden Jubilee of Queen Victoria in 1887.

ILSINGTON, showing the centre of the village before restoration in 1938. These old buildings were condemned to demolition, but saved at the last minute and restored. The old linhay in the middle was demolished, however. The children's names are, from left to right: Desmond Roberts, Hilda Roberts, George Northway, Ron Commins, Winnie Tarr, Margaret Tarr, Dick Wills (with bicycle), Charlie Heathman.

THE ILSINGTON WANDERERS CRICKET TEAM, c. 1905. In the back row, fifth from left, is Sydney Grose; in the middle row, second from left is Sydney Wills; third from left is the captain, Harry Harris.

ILSINGTON, C. 1920, showing the village post office and general stores. All these cottages were reconstructed in 1938 by Captain C.H. Quelch.

AN OUTING FROM THE CARPENTERS' ARMS, ILSINGTON C. 1920. The men were to travel by motor charabanc from Bovey Tracey. Back row, left, Harry Nickols, skilled rickmaker, thatcher, shearer and horseman on Narracombe Farm, Ilsington; he had fought in the Boer and First World Wars. Back row, right, Bill Derges, head cowman and shepherd at Narracombe, who had once been to sea. Both these men worked on Narracombe for nearly fifty years. Front row, left, Bill Redstone, horseman at Town Barton Farm, Ilsington, for farmer Bill Rowell and afterwards for the Willcocks family. Front row, centre, the driver of the charabanc, name unknown, from Bovey Tracey. Front row, right, Sam Carpenter, who farmed at the Sanctuary Farm, Ilsington. He was also the water bailiff of the Ilsington Water Supply, which supplied a large part of Ilsington parish from the reservoir at Haytor.

THE ILSINGTON CRICKET TEAM, 1938. Back row, left to right, Lewis Giles, Charlie Wills, Bill Flay, Sydney Wills (captain), Lawrence Cornish, Sydney Grose, Arthur Courtier, Bill Heathman, Bill Gill. Front row: Dick Wills, Verney Brewer, Charlie Heathman.

ILSINGTON, C. 1938. The cricket club is playing a match at Narracombe Farm, its home from 1920 to 1940. The hills on the skyline are the limestone hills of Ingsdon and Telegraph Hill; the latter was the location of one of the telegraphs that linked the country from Penzance to Portsmouth during the Napoleonic Wars.

THE WESLEYAN CHAPEL, ILSINGTON, c. 1910. In 1847 William Lambshead, aged twenty-two, returned to his native village to farm the family land at Honeywell. A devout Wesleyan, he held services regularly in his farm kitchen until 1851 when it was decided to 'build a place of their own'. Mr Lambshead gave the land, and the chapel was opened on 1 January 1852 at a cost of £70, paid for by the membership of four! Within a year the number had risen to forty and the chapel was enlarged; soon a fellowship class of over 100 was being led by Mr Lambshead.

BAGTOR MILL, ILSINGTON, c. 1900. There must have been a mill here from very early times, since Bagtor was a Saxon manor. In the picture are members of the Tickell family, who were millers here for several decades.

THE OVERSHOT WATERWHEEL AT BAGTOR MILL, ILSINGTON, c. 1900. The wheel was made in Henry Beare's machinery works at Liverton in 1875. Henry Beare came from Meeth in North Devon in the 1840s, and opened his works at Liverton because he thought the main line of the South Devon Railway was going to pass through it on the way to Plymouth. It never came, and eventually he moved to Newton Abbot. No corn is ground at Bagtor today.

ALBERT GILES, head horseman at Narracombe Farm, Ilsington, for nearly fifty years, and his son Reg, on the occasion of his winning a first prize at Ilsington Fête and Flower Show, c. 1920. The horses were Nelson and Lion.

THE ROCK INN, HAYTOR VALE, August 1896. The Burnard family and friends outside the inn. From left to right: Laurie Headly, Dorothy Burnard (with bicycle), Laurie Burnard, Mr Hext, Mrs Burnard, Mrs Preston, Charles Burnard.

IVY COTTAGE, MANATON, C. 1905. M.S. Gibbons said of the singing in St Winifred's church at this date that it 'was above the average for so small a village'. Outside was 'one of the prettiest village greens, well kept and delightfully shaded by fine old oaks, beeches and other trees. The former reminded us of Druidical remains all round us [on the moor], for if these trees do not bear mistletoe, ferns flowered in their trunks in profusion.' This was written at a time when anything old and mysterious was automatically ascribed to Druids.

MANATON, c. 1900. William Crossing held remarkably similar views to M.S. Gibbons about this part of the village, noting its 'particularly pleasing ... spacious green ... bordered with trees. At its higher or northern end, is a small inn, the Half Moon.'

CRICKET MATCH, MANATON, c. 1955.

THE CROSS AT NORTH BOVEY, 4 August 1894. For some years the shaft of this old granite cross lay in the River Bovey, but in 1829 it was recovered and repositioned by the Revd Mr Jones, the curate of the day.

THE RING OF BELLS, NORTH BOVEY, 4 August 1894. The Burnard party lined up outside were presumably in search of refreshments. They are, from left to right: Charlie Burnard (holding Mollie the horse), H. Headly, –?–, Olive, Geoffrey Reynolds, Mrs Burnard, Laurie Burnard, Nora Berrill and Dorothy Burnard. Note the duchy carriage in the background.

THE OLD INN, DREWSTEIGNTON, C. 1910. The church of the Holy Trinity is visible across the square. Walter Aggett, a farmer, was the landlord of the Old Inn, described in *Kelly's Directory* as providing 'good accommodation for tourists.'

THE OLD INN, DREWSTEIGNTON, C. 1935. Although the fabric of the village had changed little since the days of the top photograph, cars have replaced wagons and gigs, and some of the trees have disappeared from around the church. City Ales have taken over the Old Inn, and it is now run by John White.

THE SQUARE AT DREWSTEIGNTON, showing the Druid's Arms, c. 1910. Alfred Mudge was landlord, and *Kelly's Directory* of 1910 describes the Druid's as a 'family and commercial hotel and posting house; fishing tickets issued'. The pub's name was later changed to its present one, the Drewe Arms, in honour of Julius Drewe, then engaged in building the nearby Castle Drogo. Most of the thatched cottages in the square date from the sixteenth and seventeenth centuries, but note the Victorian shop on the left.

THE OLD INN, DREWSTEIGNTON, c. 1912, looking west from outside the pub. It had received a coat of whitewash since the occasion of the photograph at the top of the previous page.

THE CHURCH GATE, DREWSTEIGNTON, c. 1910. In the churchyard there is now a granite memorial to Julius Drewe of Castle Drogo, who died in 1931. It was designed by the castle's architect, Edwin Lutyens.

THROWLEIGH, August 1890. The village was recommended by Crossing as 'one from which many interesting places and objects on the border commons may be visited.'

CHURCH OF HOLY TRINITY, GIDLEIGH, C. 1900. The granite-built church dates from the fifteenth century. Note the manor house at right, with the castle ruins standing in its grounds. There is no record of this village before the twelfth century.

GIDLEIGH, 2 August 1893. The Burnard family and friends on excursion. At the front are Laurie Burnard and his mother, and behind them is Miss Palmer. Dorothy Burnard is on the box seat, with Charlie Burnard and Laurie Headly in the carriage.

GIDLEIGH CASTLE, 2 August 1893. Laurie Headley and Dorothy Burnard are outside the castle in this photograph by Robert Burnard. The building was probably the keep of a fortified manor house, and dates from c. 1300 when Sir William Prous was lord of the manor. In 1888 Crossing wrote, 'the ruins are not extensive, but are certainly interesting. There is a lower chamber, and steps by which the upper apartments are reached.'

STINIEL, CHAGFORD, August 1895. A mother and child stand in the doorway of a cottage in the tiny hamlet. In the thirteenth century it was known as 'Stenenhalle', or stone hall; this was unusual at a time when much local building was in wood.

WIDECOMBE, C. 1935. Although the parish had been going through a slow decline in its population (901 people in 1871, 704 in 1931), note the new houses in the foreground.

THE OLD INN, WIDECOMBE, C. 1920. Built in the fourteenth century, it is also believed to have served as a stannary and magistrates' court. Nearly destroyed by fire in 1977, it has now been restored.

THE CHURCH HOUSE, WIDECOMBE, c. 1945. Built of granite in 1537, it is described by Pevsner as 'the grandest in the county' and is now owned by the National Trust. In its time it has served a number of purposes, including being an ale house and a school.

CHURCH HOUSE, WIDECOMBE, c. 1950. The tree on the left of the little square fell victim to Dutch elm disease in the late 1970s.

THE GREEN, WIDECOMBE, c. 1935. Children from the village school enjoying an open-air classroom. Widecombe school dates back to 1875, when the school board became responsible for elementary education and enlarged the old National School room to government specifications.

POST OFFICE, WIDECOMBE, c. 1930. *Kelly's Directory* of 1935 has Miss May Harvey running the refreshment rooms and post office.

WIDECOMBE FAIR, c. 1930. Held on the second Tuesday in September, it was for centuries a market for large numbers of sheep, cattle and Dartmoor ponies. The fair still flourishes today, although it is now less agricultural in character.

WIDECOMBE FAIR, c. 1935. Edward Dunn of Widecombe used to act the part of Uncle Tom Cobley, the famous character from the song 'Widecombe Fair'. Here he is by the village sign, which was removed in the Second World War.

PONSWORTHY, NEAR WIDECOMBE, C. 1930. Situated in the West Webburn valley, Ponsworthy lies on the medieval packhorse route from Tavistock to Bovey Tracey.

PONSWORTHY, August 1891. Horse riders crossing the splash during an excursion. In Crossing's words, 'the hamlet, consisting of a few farmhouses and cottages and a smithy, occupies a secluded situation in a narrow valley ... it is placed in the midst of very fine scenery.'

BUCKLAND IN THE MOOR, June 1934. At this time some seventy people lived in the parish. A notable local employer was William Whitley of Buckland Court: he retained a carpenter, a foreman, a gardener and a gamekeeper from the village.

TAVISTOCK INN, POUNDSGATE, c. 1900. A meet of the South Devon Hounds. Their hunting country lay south of the Moretonhampstead – Postbridge road, and extended westward to the Dart. It's rough terrain: 'You can't ride anywhere except where you can', as the saying goes.

HOLNE, 28 December 1889. A solitary figure in an unsurfaced lane (note the wheel tracks). The photographer was Robert Burnard of Huccaby House, so we are probably looking at Mrs Burnard.

CHURCH HOUSE INN, HOLNE, 28 December 1889. Another photograph by Robert Burnard, taken on the same day as the top picture, with the same lady as the subject. Were the Burnards feeling in need of some fresh air and exercise after the Christmas festivities at Huccaby?

HOLNE VICARAGE, 22 August 1892. The house dates from 1832. The novelist Charles Kingsley (1819–75) was born in the house that previously stood on the site. Kingsley's father was curate-in-charge at Holne at the time. The writer enjoyed tremendous popularity, so much so that his historical novel *Westward Ho!* (1855) gave its name to the North Devon town.

ST GEORGE'S CHURCH, DEAN PRIOR, 13 June 1891. The poet Robert Herrick (1591–1674) held the living here from 1629 to 1647, when he was ejected by the Puritans, and again from 1662 to 1674. Although he spent thirty years at Dean, he hated Devon! He is buried in an unmarked grave in the churchyard.

SECTION TWO

Farming

NARRACOMBE SHEEP BEING DIPPED at Honeywell Farm, Ilsington, 1927. The dippers are Harry Nickols and Bill Derges. The sheep are pedigree Grey-faced Dartmoors, which were kept at Narracombe for three generations. The farm now raises pedigree Holstein cows.

JUBILEE FIELD, ILSINGTON, C. 1905. South Parks now stands here. The slopes of Pinchaford Ball and Haytor Rocks can be seen on the skyline, and nearer the then-newly-completed Haytor Hotel. Corn ricks, skillfully thatched with wheaten reed, were built side by side for threshing later in the winter by the mobile steam-threshing tackle which visited the farms. This would require several men, so it was usual for farmers to help each other. Corn ricks (of wheat, oats and barley) ceased to be built when combine harvesters came on the scene after the Second World War.

HAYTOR SHEEP SALE, HAYTOR VALE, C. 1927. The auctioneer is Ted Sawdye of Rendell & Sawdye, auctioneers of Newton Abbot. The sheep on sale were Grey-faced Dartmoors, which were kept locally. The annual Haytor sale, held in a field, stopped in about 1938.

ALBERT GILES, HEAD HORSEMAN AT NARRACOMBE, cutting oats in Queenaparks field, 1927. The horses were Lion and Bess. Bess had pulled guns in the First World War, and was deafened by them. The machine is an Albion self-binder, which cut the corn and bound it in sheaves, tying a knot in the cord. It was purchased by Dick Wills' grandfather, Charles Wills, in 1898, and was the first self-binder in the parish. Fondly known as Methuselah, it was in use until 1943.

NARRACOMBE FARMHOUSE, ILSINGTON, c. 1910. The Wills family has lived here for fourteen generations! Dick Wills, the parish historian, lives there today with his nephew's family. He writes: 'In the picture from left to right: my aunts, May Wills and Dolly Wills, my grandmother Amy Wills (born in Australia) and my grandfather Charles Wills (1854–1921), who, like his ancestors before him, had been born in the house. The dogs are Sport and Fan. My grandfather is standing under the Portugal Laurel tree, which his father "had brought home in his coat pocket from Torquay on horseback".'

SYDNEY WILLS (LEFT) AND BILL DERGES (RIGHT) stooking, or stitching, sheaves of oats in Higher Brimley Down, a Narracombe field, c. 1930. After cutting with a self-binder, the sheaves of oats were stood up in sixes, which were called stitches, where they were left until the corn and straw was really dry (about ten days in fine weather), and then it was carted to the rick. The introduction of the combine harvester removed the need for this, and the corn is now threshed at the same time as being cut.

SYDNEY WILLS, farmer at Narracombe between 1911 and 1946, pitching sheaves of oats in Lower Eastern Park field in 1944. The landgirl on the wagon was Mollie Rideout, later to become his daughter-in-law and wife to Dick Wills. Lion is in the shafts of the wagon. The oak tree behind the horse has some history: in the words of Dick Wills, 'When my grandfather was about ten, in 1864, some farm workers of Narracombe were cutting and layering this hedge. They said to him that they would leave this sapling oak as a standard and that when he was an old man it would be no bigger than his thigh. It was quite true and it was only a small tree when he died in 1921.'

HARVESTING, OR 'SAVING' THE CORN in Lower Eastern Park, Narracombe, September 1944. Tom Penellum, a farm worker, is with Darling the horse, by the empty wagon. Sydney Wills is leading Lion with the full load built by Mollie Rideout, a member of the Women's Land Army. The corn is oats.

TOM PENELLUM LEADING DARLING in Lower Eastern Park, Narracombe, September 1944. The wagon is now laden with sheaves of oats. Narracombe stopped using horses in 1949, although draught horses were used in the neighbourhood up to about 1960.

JIM HARVEY, FARM WORKER, C. 1900. He lived at Coxland, near Sigford, and worked on Higher Sigford Farm for farmer John Clark. He was born in 1860 and died in 1936.

TOR FARM, LEUSDON, C. 1910. The loose pig indicates the animal-husbandry practice of the time.

PONSWORTHY, C. 1910. A farm and outbuildings near the hamlet. Note the horse and carriage in the yard by the corner of the house.

TEIGNCOMBE MANOR HOUSE, CHAGFORD, 16 August 1889. The dilapidated Teigncombe had been one of five manors in the Chagford area at the time of the Domesday Survey in 1086.

SHEEP SALE NEAR CHAGFORD, C. 1900. During the decline of the cloth and mining industries, and despite its own ups and downs, agriculture remained (and remains) Dartmoor's single most important occupation.

LOWER COOMBE, LUSTLEIGH, C. 1910. In 1617 Nicholas Wadham, then lord of the manor of Lustleigh, conducted a survey of his domain: Lower Coombe was listed there as one of the manor farms.

THE BOVEY TRACEY HORSE-DRAWN FIRE ENGINE in action at Luscombe Farm in 1908. A similar vehicle can be seen today in the entrance to the Candy Tiles showroom at Heathfield.

LUSTLEIGH, C. 1920. Ernest Hatherley is chain-harrowing in a field beside the railway line. This is now Moor View, and is no longer farmed.

POTATO PICKERS AT UGBROOKE, CHUDLEIGH, c. 1910. Although elementary education was by now compulsory, many children needed to earn extra income for their families by working before and after school and during the holidays.

WORKERS GATHERED FOR THE HARVEST AT HAMLYN'S FARM, near Chudleigh, c. 1890. John Cobley of Rowell is standing third from left. Although there was an agricultural depression at the time, and a continuing drift from the land, farm work continued to be the mainstay of local employment.

CHUDLEIGH FARM WORKERS, C. 1890. The photograph was probably taken at Hamlyn's Farm, the home farm for the Whiteway estate near Chudleigh. John Cobley of Rowell is sitting front left. The presence of women and children indicates that it was a busy time of year, such as harvest, when extra hands were drafted in to cope with the increased workload.

TWO WORKERS AT HAMLYN'S FARM, CHUDLEIGH, C. 1890. Such men earned only two-thirds of the average industrial wage, and their housing was often poor, but the appearance of these two lends weight to the statistical evidence that at the time farm workers were among the healthiest manual workers in the country – after gardeners and engine-drivers!

Dartmoor and its Border Country

KES TOR ROCK BASIN, NEAR CHAGFORD, c. 1900. In his *Guide to Dartmoor* (1912) Crossing wrote, 'There are several rock basins on Kes Tor, but one is particularly noticeable, being by far the largest on the moor. Previous to 1856 its existence was unknown, as it had been filled with earth, probably being regarded as dangerous to sheep or cattle. In that year it was discovered by Mr Ormerod, and on its being cleared it was deemed advisable to surround it with an iron rail. Its longer diameter at the top is about $7\frac{1}{2}$ feet; the sides are sloping, the diameter at the bottom being about 2 feet. It is just over $2\frac{1}{2}$ feet in depth.' The railings have now gone.

BLACKINGSTONE ROCK, NEAR MORETONHAMPSTEAD, c. 1910. Note the figure at the foot of the steps. This great granite dome offers few foot- and hand-holds, so the steps and iron railings were built in the nineteenth century to enable visitors to enjoy the views from the top. Granite cut from the nearby Blackingstone Quarry was used in the interior construction of Castle Drogo at Drewsteignton. Worked at that time by Messrs Easton and Son, the quarry is now disused.

TOTTIFORD RESERVOIR, HENNOCK, c. 1920. By the late 1850s the growing towns of Torquay and Newton Abbot were in urgent need of improved water supplies, and in 1860 the Torquay local authority was authorized to construct the Tottiford Impounding Reservoir in the Kennick Valley near Hennock. Engineered by Messrs Easton, Amos and Sons, Tottiford was completed by 1861, and enlarged in 1866 to a capacity of 103 million gallons in an area of 31 acres.

KENNICK RESERVOIR, HENNOCK, c. 1920. Note the treeless landscape (common to all three reservoirs on this page and the next); tree planting began in earnest around this time. Kennick was built between 1881 and 1883 to supplement Tottiford's supply to Torquay. The engineer was H.M. Brunel, and it covers an area of 52 acres, and contains 194 million gallons.

TRENCHFORD RESERVOIR, HENNOCK, c. 1920. A severe drought in 1901 alerted Torquay Corporation to the need to increase yet again the water-storage capacity for the town, so Trenchford was built during the years 1903 to 1907 at a cost of £53,000. Engineered by Samuel C. Chapman, it covers 30 acres, and has a capacity of 171 million gallons.

TRENCHFORD RESERVOIR, HENNOCK, c. 1903. Workmen engaged in the construction of the reservoir between 1903 and 1907. Note the riddle-turned-banjo!

Right:
TRENCHFORD RESERVOIR, HENNOCK, 1905. The reservoir's outlet culvert is being put into position.

Below:
OLD TOTTIFORD MILL, HENNOCK, c. 1910. In 1856 the Torquay Local Board of Health had purchased the mill, its leat and the water rights, and by 1858 was supplying Torquay with water impounded in the leat. After 1861 this was superseded by supplies from the newly-built Tottiford Reservoir. William Wills shown here (seated) with his family was works manager at Tottiford in the early 1900s. The mill was demolished at around this date.

TOTTIFORD HOUSE AND WATERWORKS, HENNOCK, c. 1930. The third building from the left occupies the site of Tottiford Old Mill; note the leat, just visible below the wall on the right of the road. On the right are the filter houses; built in 1912, they contain pressure filters that were installed to purify water from the reservoirs.

TOTTIFORD WATERWORKS, HENNOCK, C. 1912. Alfred Wills, son of William Wills, the Tottiford manager, is standing beside the machinery in one of the newly-opened filter houses. The filters were installed for Torquay Corporation by the Candy Filter Company of Westminster.

TOTTIFORD WATERWORKS, HENNOCK, C. 1911. Alfred Wills on a municipal horse-drawn cart.

LUSTLEIGH CLEAVE, c. 1920. The River Bovey runs through the bottom of this narrow, steep-sided valley which — according to Crossing — was once known as Bovey Combe. Indeed, at one time a farm called Boveycombe existed in the valley, situated between Heaven's Gate and Hisley Bridge. The opening of Lustleigh railway station in 1866 turned the Cleave into a 'beauty spot', and tea rooms survived at Hammerslake until the 1930s.

IVY COTTAGE, LUSTLEIGH, C. 1930. The postcard caption would appear to be misleading, since we are looking from the railway embankment towards Pullabrook Wood and Trendlebere Down. The Wray Brook passes beneath the bridge in the foreground.

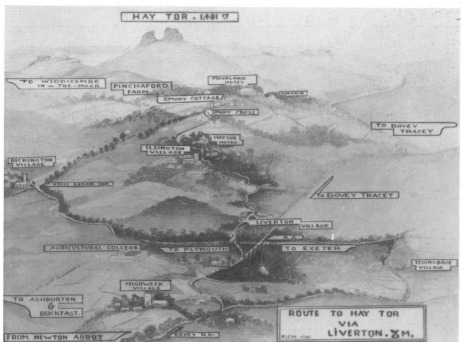

A PANORAMIC TOURIST MAP OF THE 1930s, illustrating the scenic route from Newton Abbot to Haytor, and dating from the time when the moor was beginning to attract visitors in motor cars.

HAY TOR BRAE IN THE EARLY 1900S. Now known as the Bel Alp House hotel, it was built c. 1900 on land owned by the Lyon family of Middlecott, Ilsington; the architect was Harry Lyon, who designed several other houses in the district. The house was greatly altered and enlarged in the 1930s, when Dame Violet Wills (a member of the tobacco family) lived there.

HAYTOR ROCKS, c. 1900. One of Dartmoor's most famous tors, it has long been a favourite with visitors. In 1851, a Dr Croker complained about the rock steps that had been cut 'to enable the enervated and pinguitudinous scions of humanity of this wonderful nineteenth century to gain its summit.' The notice board has now gone.

MOORLAND HOTEL, HAYTOR VALE, c. 1905. The hotel was completed in early May 1902, just before the Haytor Hotel at Ilsington; both were designed to cater for the growing tourist trade. The Moorland was built at a cost to the owners – Messrs Hellier and Lee, coaching proprietors of Bovey Tracey – of over £3,000. It originally had seventeen bedrooms and stood in ten acres of grounds, formerly part of Pinchaford Newtake. Furnishings were from Maples of London. Much of the hotel was burnt down in 1969, but it was rebuilt and reopened in December 1984 as the Moorlands Hotel.

THE MANOR HOUSE HOTEL, NEAR MORETONHAMPSTEAD, c. 1948. It was built in 1906–7 by the architect Detmar Blow as a neo-Elizabethan private residence for W.F.D. Smith, later second Viscount Hambleden. In 1929 Lord Hambleden, then a director of the company, sold the house (and 193 acres) to the Great Western Railway, who developed it into a luxurious hotel, complete with golf course and trout- and salmon-fishing rights. After nationalization, British Railways continued to run the Manor House as a hotel until it was privatized as a going concern in the 1980s.

THE LOGAN, SMALLACOMBE ROCKS, August 1896. Laurie Headly, a friend of the Burnards, is next to the logan (or rocking stone) on this granite cluster on the eastern slope of Hound Tor Combe.

FINGLE MILL, DREWSTEIGNTON, 19 August 1892. This photograph must be one of the last of the building, since it was burned to the ground in July 1893.

FINGLE BRIDGE, 19 August 1892. The Burnard family and friends on a picnic excursion. Front left, left to right: Laurie Burnard, Miss Owston and Dorothy Burnard. Back left, left to right: Olive Burnard, Mrs Burnard, Revd N. Vickers (back to camera), Carl Burnard, Charlie Burnard. Back right, Mr and Mrs Heatley. Front right, Laurie Headly.

THE TEIGN GORGE AT FINGLE BRIDGE, C. 1910. It was one of William Crossing's favourite places, giving him a 'feeling of deep gratitude to the Creator for having placed us in so beautiful a world.' Note the roof of the tea shelter, erected to cater to the needs of the increasing numbers of people who were beginning to share Crossing's feelings.

RICHARD PEEK AT FINGLE BRIDGE, C. 1900. Peek (1855–1920) was the Rector of Drewsteignton from 1895 to 1904, and much enjoyed the fishing on the Teign. His first cousin was Julius Drew, the future builder of Castle Drogo, who must have got his inspiration for the massive project during visits to his cousin's home. The foundation stone of the castle was not laid until April 1911.

THE FINGLE BRIDGE TEA SHELTER, C. 1910. Jessie Ashplant of Drewsteignton started to sell teas at this popular Teign beauty spot in 1897, and built the shelter in 1907. It lasted until 1929. Today it is the site of the Angler's Rest pub and tea rooms, and is still run by Jessie's descendants.

CASTLE DROGO, DREWSTEIGNTON, C. 1920. Workmen engaged in the construction of this huge castle-style country house, situated on a granite bluff overlooking the gorge of the River Teign. Julius Drewe (formerly Drew – he changed his name by deed poll in 1910), the romantic and wealthy founder of the Home and Colonial Stores, had commissioned the architect Edwin Lutyens to build him a granite castle near Drewsteignton, the home of his remote Norman ancestor Drogo (or Dru) de Teigne. The foundation stone was laid in 1911, but the building wasn't completed until 1930, the year before Drewe's death. The builder was Mr Lewis Bearne of Newton Abbot. Traction engines and steam lorries brought granite for the exterior from a quarry at Whiddon Park, and also from Pew Tor, to the south-west of Merrivale Quarry near Tavistock. The interior stone came from Blackingstone Quarry near Moretonhampstead. Two masons named Doodney and Cleave laid all the masonry throughout the house.

CASTLE DROGO, DREWSTEIGNTON, 1916. Well after building work started in 1911, Drewe and Lutyens were discussing and arguing over plans for the castle. In 1916 Lutyens erected a full-scale timber mock-up of the gate tower and lodges that he wanted to build (visible in the photograph, at the left). However, he failed to convince Drewe of its desirability, and the gate was never built. Today the site of the mock-up is occupied by the drive and lawns.

MELDON HILL, CHAGFORD, C. 1910. Meldon Hall, a late-Victorian house, is in the right-hand foreground. Note the absence of trees!

FERNWORTHY, NEAR CHAGFORD, 30 May 1930. On that day the Prince of Wales (the future King Edward VIII) visited the new weir and intake at Fernworthy on the South Teign. To meet increased consumer demand for water, Torquay Corporation had been authorized in 1927 to abstract water from the South Teign. By 1929 a weir across the river had been completed, along with an intake and a 16 in pipeline to Trenchford Reservoir.

FERNWORTHY DAM UNDER CONSTRUCTION. In 1934 Torquay Corporation received authority to build a reservoir and access road at Fernworthy. Work began on 16 August 1936, and the 380 million gallon reservoir opened on 22 June 1942 at a cost of £246,000.

THE B3212 MORETONHAMPSTEAD – POSTBRIDGE ROAD, C. 1931. This road probably began life as a tinners' route across the moor. The Warren House Inn, just visible in the middle distance, had flourished on the trade from the nearby Birch Tor & Vitifer and Golden Dagger tin mines, then only recently abandoned.

CULLACOMBE, SHAPLEY COMMON, 18 May 1895. George French resting in Circle A, East Enclosure at Cullacombe Head. This Bronze Age site was one of the earliest farms to be investigated by the Dartmoor Exploration Committee. Robert Burnard's album caption reads, 'Beyond white stick is hole in floor of circle supposed to have once had support in it for roof.'

CHAW GULLY, BIRCH TOR, 25 May 1894. The Revd Baring-Gould is standing in the bottom, looking east. The gully, also known as Chough Gully, is in fact artificial, being one of the old excavations associated with the Birch Tor tin mine. Mr Hannaford, the tenant of the nearby Headland Warren, once explained to Hansford Worth the origin of the gully's name: 'Chaw Gully is called after the jackdaws that used to build there; and a proper lot there were before I got tired of them and shot them out of it.'

STONE ROW, HEADLAND WARREN, C. 1894. The photograph is of the north-end stones at this prehistoric site in the parish of North Bovey. The party consisted of the Revd S. Baring-Gould, lying at left with his hat off, the Revd Gordon Gray, Dr Prowse, standing, and Mr Wilder, sitting.

GRIMSPOUND, 4 May 1894. The Revd S. Baring-Gould photographed by Robert Burnard at the entrance to the Bronze Age settlement. Grimspound had been selected by the Dartmoor Exploration Committee as its first site for archaeological investigation, and from March to June 1894 members examined eighteen buildings. In his notes Robert Burnard said that the entrance had been 'cleared of debris.'

GRIMSPOUND, 26 May 1894. Members of the Dartmoor Exploration Committee 'finishing' No. 3 Circle at the site. The Revd Baring-Gould is standing at left. While we may look askance at some of their reconstruction work, it must be remembered that these men were trying to get away from fanciful explanations of Dartmoor's past, and were among the first to examine the evidence on the ground.

GRIMSPOUND HUT CIRCLE, C. 1910. The iron railings were erected in the early years of the century to protect what was increasingly recognized as an important Bronze Age site. They were removed during the Second World War – victims of the war effort.

SOUSSONS WARREN STONE CIRCLE, 25 April 1891. Lawrence Burnard is sitting in this Bronze Age circle near Postbridge. It is now on the edge of the Soussons Down forest, originally planted in the 1940s.

FOALE'S ARRISHES, BLACKSLADE DOWN, August 1896. George French, a member of the Dartmoor Exploration Committee, sitting by the 'cooking place outside No. 1 Circle' (in Burnard's words). Early Iron Age pottery has been found at this prehistoric site near Widecombe.

EAST WEBBURN VALLEY, NEAR LEUSDON, C. 1910. According to Crossing, the river 'appears to have been anciently known as the Niprell.' It rises above Widecombe, joins the West Webburn at Lizwell Meet below Ponsworthy, and then runs into the Dart at Buckland Bridge.

DRUID, ASHBURTON, 31st July, 1905.

DEAR SIR,

The next Meeting of the TEIGN NATURALISTS' FIELD CLUB will take place on Thursday, 10th August, at Dartmeet Bridge, where the Club will assemble at 1-30 p.m. for lunch.

Conveyances are arranged to start from the Ashburton Railway Station after the arrival of the 10-47 a.m. train to take those Members who have secured seats, at 3/9 per person, returning to meet the 7-35 p.m. train.

The route from Ashburton will be by Holne Bridge and New Bridge through some romantic scenery.

After lunch a walking party conducted by the President, Mr. R. Burnard, F.S.A., will proceed up the valley of the West Dart, through the woods and by the " Pixies Cave " to Huccaby House, a distance of one mile, where Mrs. Burnard invites the Club to Tea. Members will please accept the invitation on the enclosed form to be posted not later than on Monday, 7th August.

The President will read a paper on " *A brief note on the Ancient Tenements of the Forest of Dartmoor.*"

The conveyances will come to Huccaby in time for tea and any of the party so disposed can ride instead of walking, but by so doing will miss some interesting scenery.

The return from Huccaby will probably be by Hexworthy and Holne Moor.

Places in the breaks must be secured on the attached form *not later* than by MONDAY's post, 7th August, but sooner if possible, as on Bank Holiday the country mails go out earlier than usual ; a penny stamp is required by the postal authorities on these notices & acceptances.

The CVII—S.E. sheet of the 6-inch Ordnance Map shows the country between Dartmeet and Hexworthy.

It must be understood that all places that are taken on these excursions and not used must be paid for, if required by the Treasurer.

Members may enquire for cheap tickets to Ashburton.

Yours truly,

FABYAN AMERY, *General Secretary.*

Members are reminded that " *No Dogs shall be brought to the Meetings.*

NOTICE OF A SUMMER MEETING of the Teign Naturalists' Field Club, 1905. Fabyan Amery may be seen in the two pictures opposite.

THE CLEFT ROCK, AUSEWELL WOOD, 14 January 1891. Fabyan Amery and his nephews photographed by Robert Burnard on the Cleft Rock, an old mining excavation above Holne Bridge on the Dart. (Public access is prohibited nowadays.) Amery was a keen archaeologist and naturalist, and president of the Teign Naturalists' Field Club.

AUSEWELL WOOD, RIVER DART, 14 January 1891. Fabyan Amery and his nephews are by the waterside.

CONSTRUCTING THE DAM, VENFORD RESERVOIR, HOLNE MOOR, c. 1905. Work on the thirty-three-acre scheme, designed to supply Paignton with water, began in August 1901 and finished in January 1907, at a cost of just under £120,000. The workers lived in hutments on the site, at a wage of 12s. per week, considerably more than was available in local mines or on the farms. For refreshments they walked to the Church House Inn at Holne. Building materials came to Buckfastleigh station, and were transported to the site by steam traction engines.

DARTMOOR COTTAGE KITCHEN, c. 1925. The exact location is unknown, but it has been included since photographs of domestic interiors are rare. Note the large range, the bellows and the high settle on the right.

DARTMEET BRIDGE, August 1892. The bridge was then exactly a century old, having been built in 1792 to replace the ford and clapper bridge just upstream.

DARTMEET BRIDGE, C. 1900. We are looking up the valley of the East Dart from the bridge, with the woods and plantations of Brimpts on the left. In the foreground is the medieval clapper bridge, rough blocks of granite thrown across the river to carry the packhorse traffic between Tavistock and Bovey Tracey. The clapper was washed away in severe floods on 4 August 1826, but was eventually restored by the Dartmoor Preservation Association in 1888.

SECTION FOUR

Industries

HEATHFIELD, C. 1923. Claycutters engaged in opencast ballclay extraction at Devon & Courtenay Clay Co.'s Heathfield pit. They are using thirting (thin-bladed) spades, tubils (mattock-like tools for levering up clay), and poges (spiked sticks). The name 'ballclay' is derived from this now-obsolete production method, in which the clay was cut into 31–35 lb cubes; each side was around $8\frac{1}{2}$–10 in long. Devon ballclays have been used industrially in Britain since the seventeenth century, and are now successfully marketed throughout the world.

CHUDLEIGH KNIGHTON, c. 1920. A clay worker at the entrance to the Devon & Courtenay Clay Co.'s ball-clay adit mine near the village. Mining, as opposed to the more usual opencast working, was – and is – employed wherever large amounts of waste material overlie certain high-quality clay seams.

HEATHFIELD, c. 1930. An aerial view of the Candy Tiles works. In the 1870s Frank Candy –
convinced that local clay deposits were ideal for use in the making of clay-based products –
opened the Great Western Pottery, Brick and Tile Factory beside Chudleigh Road (later
Heathfield) station. Note the sidings into the works at the right of the picture. The company
still makes tiles, but all the tall chimneys have gone, as has the group of buildings in the top
right of the factory complex, and the pottery (bottom right). The land to the left of the
arrow-straight Old Newton Road has been extensively developed, and the A38 is now a dual
carriageway.

HEATHFIELD, C. 1950. Mr Vic Towillis of the Candy pottery works. He was one of the last craftsmen throwers at Candy's as the company stopped making pottery in the 1950s.

HEATHFIELD WORKS FOOTBALL CLUB, 1931/2. A highly successful side that won Divison One of the South Devon League, and the *Torbay Herald* Challenge Cup. Back row, left to right: J. Blessington, F. Warren, J. Harris, Hy. Billinghurst, J. Hart, A. Steer, G. Burnside. Middle row: M. Bartlam, H. Weston, W. Campion, C. Caunter, F. Vallance, H. Manley, H. Osborne, S. Cann, E. Steer, F. Lupton, R. Barrett. Front row: E. Beer, W. Paddon, R. Walters, A. Beer, E. Bowden, W. Heyward, A. Steer, H. Billinhurst.

BOVEY TRACEY POTTERY, C. 1900. There had been a pottery industry in the area since at least the eighteenth century, drawing on the extensive local supplies of clay. The works in the picture were originally opened in 1836 by Divett, Buller & Co., and grew successfully during the nineteenth century, manufacturing domestic ware and souvenirs. By 1900 there were sixteen kilns in operation, and numerous workshops housing the various processes. Note the railway sidings that ran off the Newton – Moretonhampstead branch. These brought coal into the works and took away finished pottery. The pottery closed in the 1960s, and there is a question mark over the future of the few surviving buildings.

WORKERS AT BOVEY POTTERY C. 1900. By this time, the pottery was a significant local employer, with between 250 and 300 people on the books. A visitor to the works at this time, M.S. Gibbons, questioned why all the skilled tasks were undertaken by men, leaving women and girls to perform more menial jobs. She also advocated more mechanization: 'one engine should turn all the wheels employed at Bovey Factory, aye, and four times as many. With the grand supply of clay Bovey should be one of the largest potteries in England; and we ought not, within 50 miles of Bovey, to buy cups and saucers bearing the mark "Made in Germany".'

A GROUP OF WORKERS at the Higher Mill, Bovey Pottery, 1890. Here the clay was washed and slabbed before being taken to the lower pottery.

GREAT ROCK MINE, HENNOCK, c. 1943. Mining for micaceous haematite, a type of iron oxide known locally as 'shiny ore', began here in the early nineteenth century. From 1916 to 1969 the mine was operated by the Ferrubron Manufacturing Co. The ore in its natural state has a clay-like consistency, with harder lumps, and was used in the manufacture of non-corrosive paints. Owing to labour shortages, during the Second World War women were drafted in to help work the mine; note the four in the picture. Great Rock was the last working metalliferous mine in Devon, and closed in August 1969. Little remains at the site today.

GREAT ROCK MINE, HENNOCK, C. 1943. Two women workers in the interior of the crushing mill. Crushed ore is being passed through tubs and sluices to remove the waste. The pure ore was then passed on to settling tanks, and later dried to a fine powder and packaged for transit.

GREAT ROCK MINE, HENNOCK, c. 1920. The mine captain, or manager (perhaps a Mr Slatter), outside the ice-blocked entrance to an adit. Miners reached the ore lodes via a system of adits, or level passageways, most of them serviced by wagons on narrow-gauge tracks.

GREAT ROCK MINE, HENNOCK, c. 1920. Miners and workers from Great Rock on an outing to an unidentified location. Note the mine captain standing at left. The workforce of miners, washers, dryers, blacksmiths (for tool sharpening) and maintenance men rarely went above thirty in number.

CROCKHAM QUARRY WORKS, TRUSHAM, C. 1920. Rock from the Teign Valley Granite Co.'s quarry was broken down into various sizes by steam crushers, and then fed into railway trucks on sidings off the Teign Valley branch. A form of tarmacadam known as Targranix – a mixture of granite chippings and tar – was also manufactured here. The quarry is today operated by the Amey Roadstone Corporation (ARC).

CROCKHAM QUARRY WORKS, TRUSHAM, C. 1920. The railway sidings were designed to take up to 150 wagons, indicating just how busy the quarry was, and the importance of its traffic over the Teign Valley line. Rail transport from the quarry ceased in November 1967.

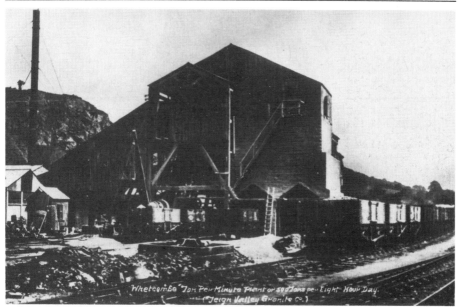

WHETCOMBE QUARRY WORKS, TRUSHAM, c. 1920. The quarry was owned by the Teign Valley Granite Co., and closed in 1931. The railway sidings survived until the 1950s. The caption vividly describes the plant's workload at its busiest: ' "Ton Per Minute Plant" or 500 Tons per Eight-Hour Day'.

SCATTER ROCK QUARRY, CHRISTOW, c. 1930. The basalt extracted here was conveyed in buckets suspended from an aerial ropeway (some of its structure is just visible in the foreground) to the railway sidings at Christow station. The quarry closed down in 1950.

SCATTER ROCK QUARRY SIDINGS, CHRISTOW STATION, *c.* 1930. The company's own rolling stock is clearly visible, as is the aerial ropeway from the quarry which fed the basalt into the wagons.

SURFACE EQUIPMENT AT BRIDFORD BARYTES MINE, 1957. Mining for barytes (known locally as brytes), a soft white mineral that occurs in vertical veins in fissures of granite, began at Bridford in the late nineteenth century. Barytes was used in the production of a number of chemicals – including barium carbonate, chloride, peroxide, etc. – that in turn formed the basis for products such as paint, glass, cosmetics and so forth. The photograph shows the surface equipment used to send the mineral from the shaft head to railway trucks at Christow station, and thence to the parent company, Laporte Chemicals Ltd, at Luton in Bedfordshire. The mine closed in August 1958, and little remains of it today.

BRIDFORD BARYTES MINE, 1957. Miners at the Laporte mine waiting for their Friday afternoon pay packet. Altogether, forty men were employed, twenty-two of them underground blasting the rock and cutting out the barytes. In a week of five nine-hour shifts they produced over 100 tons, sent to the surface in skips up a shaft hoist. A combination of dwindling reserves and market recession led to the closure of the mine in 1958. As one miner remarked at the time, 'This is almost becoming a distressed area, especially in view of the other quarries in the valley which have closed down.'

THIS MINER AT BRIDFORD BARYTES MINE in 1957 has just climbed the last few of the 750 rungs of the ladder leading from the rock surface, 600 ft below. The journey took the men about twenty minutes. The miner shown here drilled holes in the rock for explosives; in his helmet is a carbide flare, the only light below ground except around the electrically lit shafts.

COTTAGES AT HAYTOR VALE, C. 1910. These were built in 1825 for workers in the Haytor quarries, opened in 1820 by George Templer of Stover. Granite quarried at Haytor was reputedly the hardest on Dartmoor. The quarries closed down in about 1865, unable to compete against cheaper Cornish stone, although Haytor rock was used in 1919 for the construction of the Exeter war memorial. The single-workers' hostel is now the Rock Inn.

THE HOLNE BLACKSMITH, March 1892. Note the pile of discarded horseshoes to his left. Smithing was a skilled job that usually required an apprenticeship of several years. There was plenty of work: at the end of the nineteenth century there were around a million agricultural horses in England, besides those used for carriage driving and for riding. The shoes of a working horse would last for up to a month. A smith would also often be called upon to perform many other tasks, from making a gate to mending a bed.

THE TOWN MILL, BUCKFASTLEIGH, c. 1912–1913. A highly successful cloth-manufacturing business was developed here by the Hamlyn family from 1846 onwards, helping keep alive the woollen industry in the town at a time when it was dying out elsewhere in Devon. Wool was brought into the factory from farms in the surrounding area, including Dartmoor. In 1920 the mill was sold to the Co-operative Wholesale Society, who in 1932–3 built new facilities there. By the late 1960s it still employed around 300 people in the fellmongery (the processing of sheepskins), woolcombing and textile departments. In 1974, however, the mill closed and much of it was subsequently demolished. A fellmongery still survives in Buckfastleigh, along with a wool-grading and packing business.

TOWN MILL, BUCKFASTLEIGH, 20 October 1976. The end of an era came with the demolition of the chimney stack at the old CWS woollen mill. It effectively marked the passing of the large-scale woollen industry in South Devon.

BUCKFAST ABBEY, c. 1900. This photograph was taken before the modern reconstruction. On the right can be seen the neo-Gothic mansion built in 1806 by Samuel Berry, a local woollen manufacturer, on the site of the ruined Buckfast Abbey. The tall chimney and industrial buildings belong to the Lower Mills woollen factory. It was originally opened by John Berry & Co. in 1850, but it burned down in 1877, throwing 450 people out of work. It was immediately rebuilt, and concentrated on the manufacture of blankets and serge. In 1950 the nearly derelict mill was sold to the Buckfast Spinning Co., a subsidiary of Axminster Carpets Ltd. Today, all of Axminster Carpets woollen yarn is supplied from Buckfast.

SECTION FIVE

The Towns

THE CELEBRATIONS FOR QUEEN VICTORIA'S DIAMOND JUBILEE, Chudleigh, 1897. Such events were common all over the country.

CHUDLEIGH FROM THE SOUTH, c. 1910. The scene is very different today, after the building of housing estates in the fields surrounding the town.

FORE STREET, CHUDLEIGH, c. 1900. Note the Globe Inn at left; M.S. Gibbons, a writer who visited the town at about this time, was 'recommended to try the Globe Inn, and most comfortable we all found it'.

THE MARKET BUILDING, CHUDLEIGH, C. 1870. The Town Hall and the car park now occupy the site. This is one of the earliest photographs in the book, and the dilapidated appearance of the buildings suggests that Chudleigh, like many other small Devon towns, was going through a lean period. Indeed, *Murray's Handbook for Devon and Cornwall* (1859) describes it as a 'mean place'. The once-prosperous wool trade had died out as a result of competition from the steam-powered woollen mills of Yorkshire. Furthermore, the opening in 1849 of the main line railway from Exeter to Plymouth – routed away from Chudleigh – had finished off the town's stage-coach traffic.

THE SQUARE, CHUDLEIGH, c. 1910. The place looks timeless, but most of the buildings date from after the Great Fire of May 1807. As the *Globe* said at the time, 'the whole town may be termed destroyed', but fortunately there was no loss of life. An Act of Parliament forbade the use of thatch in the rebuilding programme, and the opportunity was taken to widen Exeter Way (now Old Exeter Street) up to where the fire stopped at No. 47. The building housing the West of England Insurance Office and the Lion Inn was demolished after the Second World War.

CHUDLEIGH, C. 1914. A group on one of the Teignmouth Motor Car Co.'s excursions to the moor. There was a growing public interest in visiting Dartmoor's beauty spots; guidebooks appeared each year, and William Crossing was writing regularly on moorland subjects in local newspapers.

THE PARADE, CHUDLEIGH, C. 1907. Notice all the trees. The horseman is riding west, towards Coburg. It was some sixty years since the last stagecoach had passed this way, *en route* from Exeter to Plymouth. Significantly, the first motor cars had appeared in the town around the time this photograph was taken.

THE CHUDLEIGH BRASS BAND, at a summer function, c. 1910. Many such bands were started in late-Victorian towns and villages, frequently in association with temperance societies.

CHUDLEIGH CRICKET CLUB'S 'AT HOME' FETE, 16 August 1905. This was one of the high spots in the town's social calendar for that Edwardian summer.

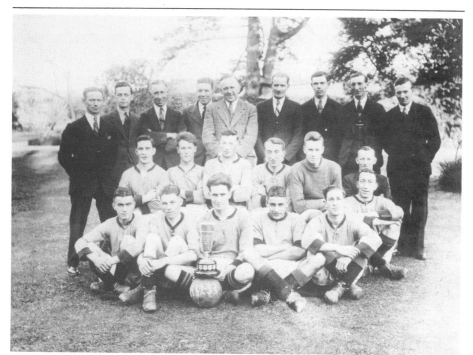

CHUDLEIGH FOOTBALL TEAM, 1932/3. The side won the South Devon League that season. There has been a team in the town since 1904, and in 1921 the club side beat Torquay United in the Devon Senior Cup.

COBURG CORNER, CHUDLEIGH, c. 1922, looking up the Parade towards the town centre. Note the numerous trees and the absence of houses.

CHUDLEIGH GRAMMAR SCHOOL, C. 1907. Mr Mackay, the schoolmaster, is standing outside with his dog Turk. There had been a charitably endowed grammar school in the town since at least the 1660s, and the building itself dates from 1668. After the school closed, pupils went to Newton Abbot.

A CHUDLEIGH CROWD CELEBRATES THE ARMISTICE of 11 November 1918 that brought the horrors of the First World War to a close. Note the US flag: America had entered the war in 1917, and there was an American military hospital in Chudleigh.

THE DEDICATION SERVICE of the Chudleigh war memorial in May 1926. The houses and the gateway to the right of Eastman's have now been demolished, providing access to the town car park.

CHUDLEIGH, c. 1920. This grocer's shop stood on the corner of Woodway Street and Old Exeter Street. It is now a private house.

CHUDLEIGH, c. 1930. Raising the church clock on the tower of the church of St Martin and St Mary.

GLEN COTTAGE TEA ROOMS, CHUDLEIGH, c. 1900. Situated near the popular Chudleigh Rock and caves, the tea rooms were ideally placed to cater for the numerous visitors to the spot.

BOVEY TRACEY AND DARTMOOR, c. 1900. A view from the tower of the parish church (St Peter, St Paul and St Thomas of Canterbury).

BRIMLEY ROAD, BOVEY TRACEY, C. 1900, part of the Victorian development of the town.

HEATHFIELD ROAD, BOVEY TRACEY, C. 1900, looking towards Dolphin Square. Note the lack of development on the right.

DOLPHIN SQUARE, BOVEY TRACEY, *c.* 1930.

BOVEY TRACEY SUNDAY SCHOOL ANNIVERSARY OUTING, 1910. The party is waiting at the railway station, *en route* to the seaside.

STATION ROAD, BOVEY TRACEY, c. 1900.

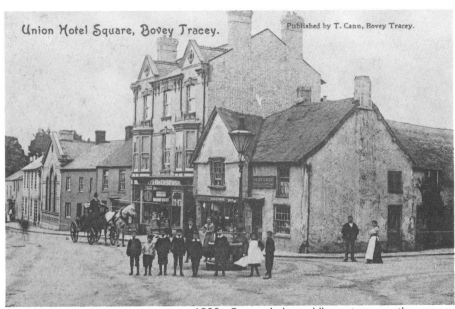

THE UNION SQUARE, BOVEY TRACEY, c. 1900. Sercombe's saddlery store on the corner subsequently became a garage; that in turn has been demolished to make way for new buildings.

The Union Square from Fore Street, Bovey Tracey.

UNION SQUARE, BOVEY TRACEY, c. 1950. Note A.E. Collins' cycle shop and garage, which had replaced Sercombe's saddlery store; also note – a sign of the times – the electricity shop.

FORE STREET, BOVEY TRACEY, c. 1904, from Union Square.

MEMBERS OF THE UNION HOTEL'S BIBLE CLASS, Bovey Tracey, 3 September 1947.

REG HODGE on the steps of his hairdressing shop, Bovey Tracey, c. 1928. Mr Hodge was responsible for starting the Bovey Boy Scout troop in 1925.

TREGONING'S GROCERY SHOP in Town Hall Place, Bovey Tracey, 1922. Stan Setters is in the white coat, and next to him is Ruby Tregoning with her five-year-old son Lance (now the town's historian).

TOWN HALL PLACE, c. 1900. Note the Town Cross, now the war memorial, outside the Town Hall of 1866.

BOVEY TRACEY TOWN HALL, 1912. Territorials parading through the town; the First World War was only two years away.

EAST STREET, BOVEY TRACEY; an early-twentieth-century view of the lower part.

MARY STREET, BOVEY TRACEY, 1905. This was a time when the street had a 'rough' reputation.

PARKE FROM MARY STREET, BOVEY TRACEY, 1930. The uninterrupted view has now gone, since much of the intervening countryside has been taken up by housing. The early-nineteenth-century Parke has become the headquarters of the Dartmoor National Park.

THE SENTRY, MORETONHAMPSTEAD, C. 1920. The town recreational area probably derived its unusual name from the word 'sanctuary', since the field was originally part of the glebe (church-owned) lands. The name certainly confused the postcard's caption writer!

GREENHILL, MORETONHAMPSTEAD, C. 1910. This is one of the oldest parts of the town. On the right, next to the church, is Greenhill School, built in 1875 and now part of the primary school. Note the cart in for repairs at the wheelwright's workshop.

THE BELL INN, CROSS STREET, Moretonhampstead, c. 1950. Wrestling matches, a thriving Dartmoor sport in the nineteenth century, used to be held in one of the pub's rooms. 'St Anne's Ales & Stouts' were supplied by the pub's owners, the St Anne's Well Brewery of Exeter (now closed down).

THE WILTS & DORSET BANK, MORETONHAMPSTEAD, c. 1928. Located on the corner of Cross Street and Station Road, the building was previously used by the grocers Boundy & Hannaford; it is now occupied by Lloyds Bank. Note the baker's handcart.

THE ALMSHOUSES, CROSS STREET, MORETONHAMPSTEAD, C. 1912. Built in 1637 to house old and poor parishioners, by 1938 they were virtually derelict and due for demolition. In that year they were bought and renovated for the town; the National Trust acquired them in 1952.

LOOKING WEST FROM THE SQUARE, MORETONHAMPSTEAD, C. 1950. The White Horse was known for many years as Gray's Hotel, after the family that owned it between 1835 and 1940.

COURT STREET, MORETONHAMPSTEAD, c. 1960. On the right is the Convalescent Home, founded in 1873 for the benefit of patients from Torquay Hospital. It closed in 1975, and is now Coppelia House, an old people's home. Just below the street light on the left is the Lucy Wills Nurses Home, built in 1902 by George Wills of Pepperdon in memory of his wife. Until the coming of the NHS it housed a nurse who was responsible for visiting the needy sick.

THE SQUARE, MORETONHAMPSTEAD, c. 1960; the view from Court Street. Mr and Mrs Cherrington ran the newsagents and sweet shop on the right from 1959 to 1985. Note the RAC road sign in the square, once a common sight in the days before local authorities assumed responsibility for traffic directions.

THE BOWRING LIBRARY AND FORE STREET, MORETONHAMPSTEAD, c. 1950. Note the Shell petrol pump on the left (now gone), and beneath it a noticeboard advertising films at the Rex Cinema. Opened in Ford Street in 1938, the Rex closed in 1957.

THE BOWRING LIBRARY AND WAR MEMORIAL, MORETONHAMPSTEAD, c. 1925. The library was built by Sir Thomas Bowring in 1901 to a design by Sylvanus Trevail; for some years it also housed the Ladies' Club and the Billiards Club. The war memorial, unveiled in 1921 by Lord Hambleden, was built on the site of the Butter Market that had been demolished in 1920.

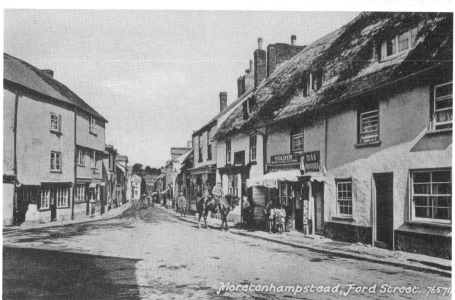

FORD STREET, MORETONHAMPSTEAD, c. 1910. Prior to 1900 it was known as Forder Street. The tobacconist and stationery shop on the right belonged to Fred Holder, an enterprising man who catered for the growing tourist trade by opening a tea room and garden.

CHAGFORD FROM RUSHFORD WOOD, c. 1904. Meldon Common is in the distance on the right, Nattadon on the left. By this date the town had adapted well to the loss of its woollen and tin industries, and had succeeded in building up a flourishing tourist trade. In 1901 William Crossing wrote that 'the primitive little place of thirty or forty years ago has become a noted resort of the tourist. During the summer season Chagford is full of visitors, and can boast of good hotels and boarding houses.'

HOLY STREET MILL, CHAGFORD, c. 1900. This old corn-mill dates from the eleventh century. Water to drive the wheel was supplied via a leat from the River Teign. Corn is no longer ground here, although the wheel was restored in 1949 to supply a local house with hydro-electricity.

CHAGFORD FROM THE SOUTH, c. 1935. Note the new houses in the foreground.

CHAGFORD SQUARE, c. 1930. The view is towards High Street.

THE OCTAGONAL MARKET HOUSE, CHAGFORD, 1908. It was built in 1862, the gift of Revd Hayter George Hames, to replace an older building nicknamed 'the Shambles'. The rector sponsored many improvements to the town, including the provision of a proper drainage system and water supply, and the installation of gas in 1869. Chagford later became (in 1891) one of the earliest towns to boast electric street lighting, generated by water power.

HIGH STREET AND ST MICHAEL'S CHURCH, CHAGFORD, c. 1935. The church dates from the fifteenth century and was much restored in the nineteenth century. The Three Crowns Hotel was built in the early sixteenth century as the town house of the Whiddon family, then the largest local landowners. In 1643, during the Civil War, Sydney Godolphin, the young Cavalier poet, died at the house from a musket wound. Tradition has it that the hotel is still haunted by his ghost. Clarendon, the royalist historian, said that his death brought 'ignominy . . . upon a place which could never otherwise have had a mention in the world'.

AUTUMN SALE OF BREEDING EWES, Chagford Market, c. 1900. Markets and fairs continued to take place regularly in the town, although the income was falling away. Livestock could now be driven to Moretonhampstead railway station, where there were cattle pens, and transported by train to market in Newton Abbot.

NEW STREET, CHAGFORD, C. 1917. The town's road cleaner at work with his donkey-hauled dust-cart. This is one of the oldest streets in the town, and some buildings date back to medieval times.

Chagford, Old House.

LOWER STREET, CHAGFORD, C. 1910. On the near left is the Bishop's House, a late medieval building with a seventeenth-century porch. It is said to have been used by the bishops of Exeter on their visits to the town.

RUSHFORD MILL FARM, CHAGFORD, c. 1910. The water-powered corn mill was in operation for 400 years, closing down in the nineteenth century. It was one of four such mills in the parish, the last to close being Sandy Park Mill in 1917. Between 1933 and 1936 volunteers built a public swimming pool on the site of the old Rushford mill pond. It is still in use today.

THE BULLRING, ASHBURTON, c. 1900, looking from West Street towards East Street. Bull baiting was once a popular spectacle in the town centre, and it is said that stagecoaches tailored their timetables to fit in with the events. The sport was made illegal in 1835.

THE BULLRING, ASHBURTON, c. 1950. The buildings themselves have changed little since 1900, and they are still used primarily as shops. The presence of cars, the garage, and people's clothes are the obvious differences. Ashburton's population (2,704) was just beginning to grow again, having been on the decline since 1831.

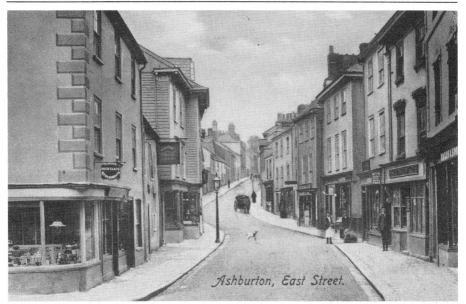

EAST STREET, ASHBURTON, c. 1910. This street once formed part of the main stage-coach route between Exeter and Plymouth, but the opening in the 1840s of the main-line railway between the two cities – by-passing Ashburton – had killed the busy trade. The arrival of the Ashburton branch line in 1872 did not bring the hoped-for revival of prosperity.

EAST STREET, ASHBURTON, c. 1900, looking west to the town centre. The Golden Lion on the left had once catered for the stage-coach trade and, in the words of M.S. Gibbons, a late-Victorian traveller: 'The hotel is roomy, with capital accommodation, and is situated in a charming garden'.

ST LAWRENCE'S LANE, ASHBURTON, c. 1910. Note the gas street light, installed in the mid-nineteenth century, and supplied with gas from the works near the station.

ST LAWRENCE'S LANE, ASHBURTON, c. 1910. The sixteenth-century tower of St Lawrence's Chapel is in the mid-distance. For four centuries – from the 1540s to 1938 – a grammar school was housed in the chapel. The building is now in the care of the Dartmoor National Park.

NORTH STREET, ASHBURTON, C. 1910. The view towards the Bullring.

NORTH STREET, ASHBURTON, C. 1900. Opposite the Town Arms is the Market Hall (now the Town Hall), built in 1848 by Lord Clinton to replace the Bullring's Old Market House. The upper end of North Street was a slum area in Victorian times; the woollen industry had collapsed, and farm work paid poorly.

NORTH STREET, ASHBURTON, C. 1939. The buildings had altered little since 1900, but the growth in motor transport required a traffic controller.

BUCKFAST ABBEY CHURCH, 1937. Although the church was consecrated in 1932, work on the tower did not finish until 1938.

THE RECONSTRUCTION OF ST MARY'S ABBEY CHURCH, BUCKFAST, C. 1930. One of the South West's greatest Cistercian monasteries had stood here in medieval times, but it was allowed to fall into ruins after the Dissolution of 1536–9. In 1882 a community of French Benedictines acquired the site, and decided to rebuild the great abbey. Work on the church, designed by F.A. Walters, began in 1907, undertaken entirely by a small group of monks under the direction of a master mason. Twenty-five years later, in 1932, the church was consecrated by Cardinal Bourne, the Archbishop of Westminster.

BOTTOM END OF FORE STREET, BUCKFASTLEIGH, 1952. On the left is the Valiant Soldier public house (now closed), and then a cafe that was run in tandem with a garage business. It is now a restaurant. In the distance is the ivy-covered Bridge House, which stands on Dammerell's Bridge.

THE SALMON LEAP, DART BRIDGE, Buckfastleigh, c. 1935. A popular pub on the old road from Exeter to Plymouth.

SOUTH BRENT, c. 1900. Another old wool town, the population now numbered some 1,500. William Crossing, the great Dartmoor authority, lived in Brent until the 1890s. When he was a young man his father had appointed him supervisor of the family mill there. In this he was unsuccessful, since the mill failed in the 1870s. Crossing generally preferred to be out exploring the moor rather than following office routine!

SOUTH BRENT CATTLE SALE, c. 1900. A contemporary directory described Brent thus: 'Formerly a market town, and still has two annual fairs, on the last Tuesdays and Wednesdays in April and September, the former called the lamb, and the latter the goose fair, but both are extensive marts for sheep, cattle and horses, held "under the glove", a glove being suspended on a pole during the fairs. On the last Tuesdays in February and August, good cattle markets are held.' Compare the scene with that in the photograph below.

THE ANCHOR HOTEL, SOUTH BRENT, c. 1955.

SOUTH BRENT HORSE MARKET, *c*. 1900. Ponies and horses from the surrounding district were brought in for sale in the street, a custom that has now gone. The Pack Horse Hotel is still there, its name a reference to the days when pack horses were the main means of transport on the moor. Again, compare the scene with that in the photograph below.

THE PACK HORSE HOTEL, SOUTH BRENT, in the late 1950s.

SECTION SIX

Transport

BRENT STATION, c. 1900. Situated on the Great Western Railway's main line from Exeter to Plymouth, the station was opened shortly after the railway itself in 1848. In 1893 Brent became the junction station for the new Kingsbridge branch line (note the reference on the station nameboard). Both Brent station and the branch have now closed.

WIDECOMBE, C. 1895. Dorothy Burnard and a companion in the miller's cart. Wheeled transport had been a rarity on the moor until the construction of proper roads in the late eighteenth and early nineteenth centuries. Prior to that time, the packhorse was the normal carrier of goods.

DOLPHIN HOTEL, BOVEY TRACEY, C. 1900. A four-in-hand team prepares to take a party of excursionists on to the moor.

HEATHFIELD STATION, 9 June 1921. In the photograph we are looking north towards Bovey Tracey. Situated on the GWR's Newton Abbot – Moretonhampstead branch (finished 1866), Heathfield opened as Chudleigh Road station in 1874 to handle anticipated traffic from the proposed junction with the Teign Valley branch (opened 1882), seen here curving away to the right beyond the signal box. Note the siding at left serving Candy's brick and tile works. The Moretonhampstead branch closed to passengers on 2 March 1959, but Heathfield station remained open for freight until 3 December 1967. Today, the line survives as a freight-only route to the Heathfield industrial estate.

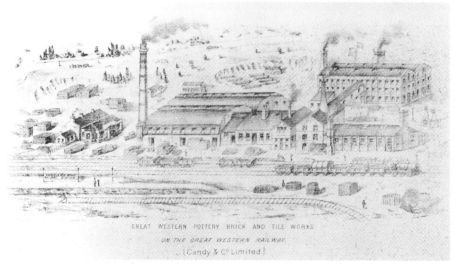

GREAT WESTERN POTTERY BRICK AND TILE WORKS

ON THE GREAT WESTERN RAILWAY

[Candy & Cº Limited]

CANDY'S HEATHFIELD WORKS, c. 1882. Note the track laid to broad gauge (7 ft); it was converted to standard gauge (4 ft 8½ in) in 1891. The station name has not yet been changed to Heathfield. The goods train is facing north on the Moretonhampstead branch, and in the foreground is the Teign Valley branch. (See also pages 91–3.)

BOVEY TRACEY STATION, 1920. The charabancs in the approaches would indicate that considerable business must have been expected, judging by the number of waiting vehicles. The destination board on the left-hand charabanc reads 'Haytor Rocks'; that on the right reads 'Bovey Tracey Becky Falls Manaton'.

FLOODS AT BOVEY TRACEY STATION, 1930. An important intermediate station on the GWR's Moretonhampstead branch, it opened in 1866 and closed to passengers in 1959. Freight services were withdrawn in 1970, and the surviving buildings converted to commercial use. The track bed from Bovey pottery to just north of the former station is today taken up by the Bovey Tracey by-pass.

STATION STAFF AT BOVEY TRACEY, 1958. This photograph was taken just before it closed to passenger traffic.

LUSTLEIGH STATION, c. 1955. Like other stations on the Moretonhampstead branch, Lustleigh lost its passenger service in March 1959, although goods trains continued to run through the disused station until 1964. The station is now a private house.

GWR TRAIN, MORETONHAMPSTEAD STATION, *c.* 1920. Built originally to accommodate broad-gauge trains (7 ft against the standard gauge of 4 ft $8\frac{1}{2}$ in), the station buildings were generously proportioned, and at its busiest the terminus of the twelve-mile branch from Newton Abbot provided employment for a fair number of local people. Falling revenues led to the complete closure of the station on 6 April 1964, and the site is now occupied by the busy Thompson's road-haulage depot.

MORETONHAMPSTEAD STATION, *c.* 1920. An interesting view of the cattle pens at the western end of the branch terminus. Cattle were a regular part of the freight mix on the line, and the picture reminds us just how useful the railway was in the days before effective road transport.

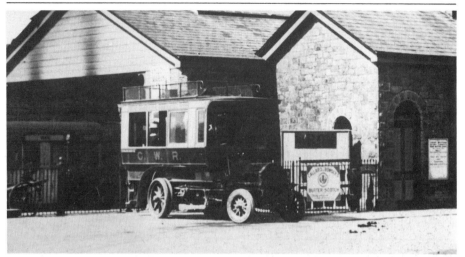

MORETONHAMPSTEAD STATION, c. 1910. A good view of the GWR's Milnes Daimler omnibus that operated the route between Moretonhampstead and Chagford. The GWR was one of the pioneers of motor-bus operations in Britain.

A GREAT WESTERN RAILWAY MILNES DAIMLER OMNIBUS in Chagford Square, c. 1910. The town was never on any railway line, the nearest station being five miles away at Moretonhampstead, the terminus of the GWR's twelve-mile branch line from Newton Abbot that had opened in 1866. A privately owned horse-drawn omnibus operated a feeder service between Chagford and Moretonhampstead until April 1906, when the GWR introduced its own motor bus on the route. Note the Perrott name on the shop-front at left. James Perrott (died 1895) started the fishing-tackle and horse-and-carriage hire business to cater for the holiday trade, and he guided many visitors to remote parts of the moor. In 1854 he built the first Dartmoor 'letterbox' at Cranmere Pool; after his death his four sons continued the business.

CHAGFORD SQUARE, C. 1905. These two 32 hp Clarkson steam omnibuses were built at Chelmsford, and started plying between Chagford and Exeter as a connection for the London & South Western Railway in the summer of 1905. Registered LC690/1 they each seated twenty passengers and were silent and smooth in operation, could climb hills without the use of a clutch or gears and had lively acceleration. In placing the driver high up, the manufacturers claimed that he was 'at great advantage in being able to see over the hedges when coming to crossroads, thus lessening the risk of collision with other vehicles!' Both vehicles were withdrawn on 15 January 1908.

CHUDLEIGH STATION, 11 June 1921. Located on the Great Western Railway's Teign Valley branch (from Newton Abbot to Exeter via Heathfield), the station opened in October 1882. It closed to passengers on 7 June 1958, but freight operations – mostly coal and oil – continued until 3 December 1967. Today, this section of the line is occupied by the A38 dual carriageway.

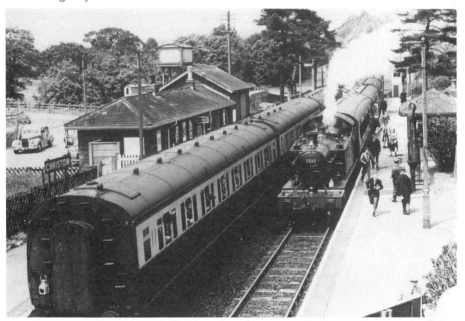

CHRISTOW STATION, 7 June 1958. The last day of passenger-train operations on the Teign Valley branch. Locals were unhappy about the closure, and schoolchildren paraded with placards against the decision. The station remained open for goods traffic to Heathfield until 1 May 1961.

GWR STATION, ASHBURTON, C. 1910. Opened in St Lawrence's Lane in 1872 as the terminus of a nine-mile branch from Totnes, it closed to passengers in 1958, and to freight in 1962. In 1969, Ashburton reopened as part of the preserved Dart Valley Railway, but it was forced to close again in October 1971, as the track between Buckfastleigh and Ashburton was dismantled to make way for the A38 dual carriageway. The building is now a garage.

ASHBURTON BY-PASS, C. 1933. The increase in motor traffic throughout the 1920s meant that Ashburton's narrow streets became intolerably congested. In 1933, to relieve the pressure, the A38 main road was diverted to the south of the town. It was upgraded to dual-carriageway status in the early 1970s.

DOLPHIN SQUARE, BOVEY TRACEY, c. 1910. Cars outside Moir & Davie's garage.

CHUDLEIGH CHARABANC OUTING, c. 1925. Operated by Bulpins of Newton Abbot, the 'Pride of the Moor' service started in the early 1920s, part of the post-war boom in motor transport that enabled people to visit the moor in increasing numbers.

ACKNOWLEDGEMENTS

I am indebted to a host of people for their kindness and co-operation during the compilation of this book. My task would have been impossible without them. The individuals and organizations listed here supplied the photographs (and, in many cases, information about them) on the following pages:

Margaret Bonnell: 110b, 117b; British Geological Survey: 97, 98; Steve Carreck of Watts Blake & Bearne: 89, 90; Gwyneth Chard: cover, 53, 135, 136, 137, 139, 155b; Chudleigh Amenity Society: 12, 13a, 56, 57, 58, 111, 113a, 114b, 117a, 118, 119a, 159b; Bob Crawley: 156; Elizabeth Earle of The National Trust: 74b, 75a; Philip Eldridge: 88; Joan and Eddie Ellis: 15, 16a, 17, 19, 20, 54a, 55; David German: 11, 18b, 28, 29b, 36, 37, 38, 41, 51b, 52a, 60, 66, 67a, 70, 77b, 87a, 108, 121a, 123a, 128, 129b, 130a, 132b, 133, 134, 138, 140, 141, 142, 143, 144a, 158b; Peter Gray: 153b, 157b; Peter Hughes of ARC Trusham: 100, 101, 102; Wilf Joint: 107b; Graham Lee: 109, 110a, 112, 113b, 114a, 115, 116; Mrs Lester: 13b, 75b, 83, 134b; Graham Lucas of Candy Tiles: 91, 92, 93, 151b; LGRP Collection: 151, 154b, 155a, 157a, 158a; Jack Price: 31, 32, 33a, 72b, 73, 74a; Lady Sayer: 27b, 30, 33b, 34b, 35, 40b, 42, 43, 44, 52b, 71, 72a, 78, 79, 80, 81a, 82, 84, 85, 87b, 106, 150a; David St John Thomas: 154a; The Times: 39a; Lance Tregoning: 54b, 94, 95, 96, 119b, 120, 121b, 122, 123b, 124b, 125, 126, 127, 150b, 152, 153a, 159a; Peter Webb: 34a, 39b, 40a, 67b, 81b, 86, 107a, 129a, 130b, 131, 132a, 144b, 145, 146a, 147b, 148b; Michael Wells of Torquay Natural History Society: 103, 104, 105a; West Country Studies Library: 2, 14, 29a, 59, 68b, 146b, 147a, 148a, 149; Dave Wills: 61, 62, 63, 64, 65, 76, 77a, 99, 124a; Dick Wills: 16b, 18a, 21, 22, 23, 24, 25, 26, 27a, 45, 46, 47, 48, 49, 50, 51a, 68a, 69, 105b.

The sources of quotations from William Crossing's writings are *Gems in a Granite Setting* (by kind permission of Devon Books) and *Crossing's Guide to Dartmoor* (by kind permission of David & Charles). The comments by M.S. Gibbons come from *'We Donkeys' on Dartmoor*, published by Henry S. Eland of Exeter, c. 1900. I also owe a great deal to the works of many local historians; unfortunately, the pressure of space dictates that I cannot acknowledge them individually.

I should also like to thank Gareth Griffiths of Photography 2000 for his excellent copying of valuable old prints; Ethan Danielson for the map; John Weir of the Dartmoor National Park for reading the captions (any errors remain my responsibility); and Judith Harvey, Simon Thraves and Louise Kirby of Alan Sutton Publishing for their heroic patience over a long period. Finally, I want to thank the members of my family for their constant support and encouragement.